D0390150

NORTH AMERICAN INDIAN
MEDICINE PEOPLE

OREGON EPISCOPAL SCHOOL
LOWER SCHOOL LIBRARY
6300 S.W. Nicol Rd.
Portland, OR 97223

Withdrawn

NORTH AMERICAN INDIAN MEDICINE PEOPLE

KAREN LIPTAK

FRANKLIN WATTS
NEW YORK/LONDON/TORONTO/SIDNEY
A FIRST BOOK/1990

Frontis: A nineteenth-century painting shows
a medicine man in the role of healer.

Cover photograph courtesy of: Hudson's Bay Company
Archive/Provincial Archive of Manitoba

Photographs courtesy of: New York Public Library,
Picture Collection: pp. 2, 8, 13, 18, 28, 34 (National
Geographic Society), 37, 39, 47; Hudson's Bay Company
Archive/Provincial Archive of Manitoba: pp. 11, 12;
Museum of the American Indian, Heye Foundation:
pp. 17, 32, 51; The Bettmann Archive: pp. 20, 24;
American Museum of Natural History: p. 56 top;
Photo Researchers: pp. 42 top (Marion Patterson),
42 bottom (Emil Meunch), 45 top (Tom McHugh/Denver
Museum of Natural History), 58 (Ulrike Welsch);
The University Museum, University of Pennsylvania:
p. 45 bottom (Edward S. Curtis); Jeff Greenberg
Agency: p. 56 bottom (Betty Groskin).

Library of Congress Cataloging-in-Publication Data

Liptak, Karen.

    North American Indian medicine people / Karen Liptak.
      p. cm. — (A First book)
    Includes bibliographical references.
    Summary: Describes the healing techniques used by
various American Indian tribes and explains the
theories and beliefs behind these practices.
    ISBN 0-531-10868-6
    1. Indians of North America—Medicine—Juvenile literature.
[1. Indians of North America—Medicine.] I. Title. II. Series.
E98.M4L57 1990
615.8′82′08997—dc20   90-12337 CIP AC

First Paperback Edition 1992
0-531-15640-0

Copyright © 1990 by Karen Liptak
All rights reserved
Printed in the United States of America
5 4 3

A special thank-you to Carol Locust, Ph.D., director of training at the Native American Research and Training Center in Tucson, Arizona, and to Martha Kreipe de Montaño, for patiently reviewing this work and offering helpful criticism.

North American Indians are currently called American Indians as well as Native Americans. I have chosen to use "American Indians" in the title to help readers find the book more readily—as it is the more traditional term—and to reflect the feelings of American Indians as they were voiced in a survey at a recent Reno, Nevada, Indian powwow.

CONTENTS

MEDICINE MEN AND WOMEN

In the daily lives of the North American Indians, medicine men and women have played—and are still playing—an important role. American Indians generally believe that medicine people have the power to help them in their time of need. By "power" they mean energy of a spiritual nature.

But not all tribes have the same kind of medicine people. Some tribes, like the Yurok of California, have only medicine women. Other tribes have only medicine men. Some tribes, like the Hopi and the Apache of the American Southwest, have many different medicine people, each with their own specialty. Other groups have one medicine person to do everything, from counseling people to healing wounds and disease.

Medicine people aren't limited to healing sick and injured people. In most tribes, they are also called upon to predict the future and to help tribal members

A Blackfoot medicine man
with his history in pictures
in the background.

have good luck in hunting and planting. Medicine people are also asked to influence the weather.

The Ojibwa, also known as the Chippewa, are a major tribe in the Great Lakes region. Corn was an important crop for the tribe. Black Tongue, an Ojibwa medicine man, was known for his ability to sing to the corn and make it grow. When the cornfields were dry, the Ojibwa poured water over Black Tongue's head as he sang his song and, it is reported, it always rained.

Among most tribes, medicine men or women may also be asked to conduct ceremonial feasts and dances for the tribe or for individuals. These include everything from birth and burial rites to sporting events.

A specially trained medicine man in the Apache tribe leads the singing in the Sunrise Dance. This four-day ritual is performed for a girl when she passes from childhood to womanhood, usually between the ages of twelve and fourteen. The girl is dressed in a beautiful buckskin costume. During the ceremony, many people shower her with cattail-plant pollen, which is considered holy to the Apache.

Ball games are a favorite tribal sport for the Cherokee of the American Southeast. The medicine person presides over these events. On the morning of each game, he or she says special prayers as the players take a ritual sweatbath (see page 41), followed by a dip in the cold water of the river. Then the medicine person scratches each player with a special comb containing seven teeth. Seven is the Cherokee's sacred number. The scratching, like the sweatbath and cold-water plunge, are part of the traditional preparation for the ball game.

The medicine person presided over many kinds of ceremonies, including ball games.

The Bear Dance was a major ceremony for
the Sioux of the Great Plains. Led by the tribe's
medicine man, this dance was performed before
a bear hunt to ensure its success.

Medicine people are often respected and even
feared by their tribal members. They are respected
because they assist the ill to become well with their
"good medicine." They are feared because they can
also use their power to cause illness. This is called
"bad medicine."

In an 1832 painting, a medicine person leads a Mandan
Bull Dance, asking for plentiful herds of buffalo.

In the past, payment for a medicine person's services was given in such items as buffalo hides, dried meat or other food, or utensils. It was not unusual for medicine people to become very rich.

BEING HEALTHY

The North American Indian generally believes that you are healthy if your body, mind, and spirit are in harmony. Harmony is a peaceful state that puts you "at one" with the universe.

Whatever the state of your body, Native Americans believe that you are in harmony if your basic attitude lets you live in peace. Once such harmony is yours, the daily ups and downs of life won't bother you.

American Indians believe that there are two main causes of illness: natural causes and unnatural ones. Natural causes come from the patient. For instance, the most common natural cause of illness is violating one of a tribe's taboos or treating sacred objects with disrespect.

Each tribe has its own set of taboos. To the Apache, the bear, owl, and eagle are considered taboo animals; even "sitting" near one will cause a problem. Among the Hopi, a woman will break a taboo if she fishes, swims, or eats fish while she is pregnant. Mistreating an animal is also a taboo to the Hopi. So is failing to help someone in need.

Unnatural causes of illness come from bad forces outside of someone's body. Such forces can affect a person whose spirit is too weak to fight them. These forces are usually known as witchcraft.

American Indians believe that when disease strikes—from either natural or unnatural causes—a foreign object has invaded the patient's body. Whether it came from violating a taboo or from being "witched," special medicine is needed to remove the deadly object.

This special medicine comes from the medicine person. Often, just knowing that the medicine person is on the way helps patients feel hopeful, which may speed their recovery.

CHOOSING AND TRAINING MEDICINE PEOPLE

Medicine people are chosen in a variety of ways. In some tribes, the role is a family tradition passed down from a parent or grandparent who is a medicine person. In other tribes, elders who aren't blood relatives can choose someone to follow in their footsteps after seeing in that person's actions or words a "sign" of good medicine power.

Elsewhere, someone may be allowed to become a "doctor" if he or she has the price a practicing medicine person requires to take on an apprentice. But perhaps the most common way for American Indians to become medicine people is to be guided to that profession in a dream.

Dreams and Vision Quests

For many American Indians, the dreams to become a medicine person come during a vision quest, which many Indian boys still go on when they are about twelve years old. In some tribes, girls also go on vision quests. These are solitary trips taken to find a purpose and guide in life.

By the time a Native American youngster begins a vision quest, he or she is well prepared to survive alone in the woods for a few days. Before setting off, each youngster goes through a morning cold-water ritual and then leaves all family behind to head into the woods alone. There he or she remains for the next few days without any food or water, waiting for a vision to come. This vision brings the youngster a spirit

A medicine woman of the Yurok of California.

helper for life. The spirit helper might appear in the form of an animal or a person.

Usually, if the child has a vision that indicates that he or she has medicine power, the family will consult a local medicine person about the child's future training.

For a certain fee, the medicine person will teach the child his or her secrets. The price is sometimes steep, since the training takes much time and patience on the part of the medicine person. The student has much to master. There are many chants, songs, and ceremonies to memorize. By saying a chant incorrectly, a medicine person can endanger a patient's life.

The student also has to learn the names and locations of many medicinal plants and also must learn exactly how to gather and prepare them. If the student accidentally uses a poisonous plant or gathers a good medicine plant without the proper ceremony, the patient may be hurt, or even killed.

The Mandan medicine man
gained his power through dreams
and visions; his instruction came
from a more experienced
medicine person.

Among North American Indians of Alaska, a medicine
man is shown conducting a healing ritual.

Many tribes have additional training for their medicine people. Among the Eskimo, the medicine person has to memorize the secret, sacred name for each bone of the body. This name is known only to the medicine people. They also must memorize tribal histories and proverbs to recite in healing rituals.

The Comanche are a tribe of the American Great Plains. It is traditional that an unmarried Comanche woman can't become a medicine person on her own. However, a married woman can gain healing power by helping her medicine man husband. Only after his death can the wife practice on her own.

THE MIDEWIWIN, THE GREAT MEDICINE SOCIETY OF THE OJIBWA

The Ojibwa, or Chippewa, are a major tribe of the Great Lakes region. The Midewiwin (mee-DAY-wee-win) is a medicine society to which many villages of the Ojibwa belong. This medicine society is a group of medicine people, known as Mides—singular, mide (mee-DAY).

The songs, chants, prayers, and rituals of the medicine society are said to come from the spirit

Winabozo, the Great Rabbit. Winabozo directed the otter to teach the people how to make their rattles and drums. During ceremonies, the people shake the rattles and beat the drums.

In order to join the Great Medicine Society of the Midewiwin, a vision of a helping spirit must appear to a young male and advise him to join. Then, if he can afford the fee and is accepted by the society, one of the members is assigned to teach him about herbs and the society's traditions.

For many years the student and teacher go out into the woods together. There, the student learns about all the plants he will use in his work. He is taught how to make an offering of tobacco to the spirits for each medicinal plant he gathers. First, he pulls up the plant. Then he throws a bit of tobacco into the hole that is left behind. The hole is covered with leaves. Finally, the student memorizes the chant that goes with the gathering of each plant. It takes about seven years of study before a student Mide is ready to be initiated into the Midewiwin Society.

Initiation into Midewiwin

More than one Mide is initiated into the Midewiwin Society at the same time. A hundred years ago, a messenger would carry news of the upcoming event to the surrounding Ojibwa villages, for initiations were always exciting times for the tribe.

The ceremony was held in the Midewigan, or Medicine Lodge. This was a very large wigwam built in the center of a large field. Days before the initiation, people from other villages began arriving to set up their shelters around the Midewigan. These shelters were often made from the bark of the birch tree.

On the ceremony day, the families of the young Mide initiates hung gifts on poles inside the Midewigan. These gifts were for the members of the Mide council. Meanwhile, each initiate took a ceremonial sweatbath to cleanse his body and clear his mind. These ritual sweatbaths were taken in special shelters called sweat lodges.

The Mide society had various levels, each level represented by its own face paint. However, the initiates' faces were bare of paint.

The beating of a drum announced the start of the ceremony. A typical ceremony might follow this pattern:

While the drum beating continues, the initiates and four Mides, including the chief Mide, walk around the Midewigan four times. They chant as they walk. Then, one by one, each initiate gets a turn.

Each Mide now points his medicine bag at the initiate. These bags are made from otter skin, and they

The Ojibwa wait outside the Chief Midé's wigwam
for the end of the initiation ceremony.

contain many sacred items. The most sacred item of all is the cowrie, a seashell that is the main emblem of the Midewiwin Society. Each Mide removes a seashell from his bag and throws it at the initiate. In this way, each Mide is showing a willingness to transfer some of his own power to the new Mide.

As each cowrie shell is tossed at him, the initiate staggers and reels a little more. Finally, he falls to the ground.

One by one, each Mide touches the initiate with his medicine bag. But the initiate remains on the ground until the chief Mide orders him to stand up. Then he is given a medicine bag of his own.

Now it is the initiate's turn. He reaches into his bag and draws out one seashell at a time. These shells he throws at the Mides. One by one the Mides collapse, as if dead. Then the initiate bends over the seemingly lifeless Mides and touches them with his new medicine bag.

Slowly, the "dead" Mides begin to revive.

The initiate has proven his medicine power. Now he can have his face painted to show his own level in the Great Medicine Society of the Midewiwin.

A feast follows every initiation. Afterward there are speeches and performances by the Mides. Finally, the chief Mide excuses himself to go into a small wigwam near the Midewigan. The people outside his tent hear a drum begin beating inside. Faster and faster it beats. The walls of the Mide's tent begin swaying back and forth. Strange howls and mumbled voices are heard. The spirits have arrived! The Ojibwa, scared yet grateful, remain absolutely still until all the noises within the tent have ceased.

Like all initiation ceremonies, this is a memorable one. On this night, the Ojibwa are once again reminded of how powerful their Great Medicine Society is.

NAVAJO CEREMONIES AND SAND PAINTINGS

The Navajo, one of North America's largest Indian tribes, live in the Four Corners area of Arizona, Colorado, Utah, and New Mexico—a land of strikingly beautiful, many-colored sands. Navajo medicine men are highly esteemed within the tribe. And sand paintings play a major role in many Navajo healing ceremonies. Each sand painting is an intricate work made primarily from colored sandstone that has been crushed into a fine powder. Over a thousand different sand paintings are used by the Navajo.

Before a healing ceremony can be performed, a diagnosis is made of the patient's problem. Then a specific healing chant must be selected. Different chants serve different purposes. Chants also vary in length, and in expense to the patient.

The shortest and most general chant is called Blessing Way. It lasts for two days and may be performed without a sand painting. On the other hand, Night Chant lasts nine days and includes eight or nine sand paintings, depending on the version. Some other Navajo healing chants are called Hail Chant, Shooting Chant, and Big Star Chant.

Navajo chants tell stories about legendary heroes or heroines who go through daring adventures to reach the gods and obtain a cure for their ailment. The figures used in sand paintings symbolize the people and actions in the chanted myths.

A Navajo healer studies for many years to become a chant singer and a sand painter. (It is considered impressive to memorize four chants in a lifetime.) On a set day, generally at sunrise, the healer begins creating the necessary sand painting on the floor of the ceremonial hogan (earth house).

The healer makes no first sketches. Even the most elaborate sand paintings are created from memory. He "paints" by letting streams of crushed colored

sand slide down between the thumb and index finger of his right hand. The result may look simple, although it takes many hours and much skill to achieve.

Five main colors, each with its own meaning, are used.

White symbolizes the east. It also represents dawn, spring, youth, and the higher world. New beginnings and spiritual purity are white as well. White can stand for evil forces, too, such as White Thunder and Great White Serpent.

Black symbolizes the north. It also represents night, winter, old age, death, and witchcraft. Although Black Clouds and Black Thunder may seem threatening, they also bring life-giving rains.

Blue symbolizes the south. It also represents summer, middle age, and spiritual happiness. On the negative side, the Blue Star brings misfortune, and the Great Blue Snake causes epidemics.

Yellow symbolizes the west. It also stands for twilight, autumn, and the maturing of life.

Red is the only color that doesn't stand for a direction. It represents power, life-force, and danger.

The medicine man allows the colored sand to trickle down between his thumb and first finger to form the designs of the sand painting.

Around each sand painting there is usually a protective border, such as the Rainbow Guardian. And the middle of the painting often has a reference point, such as a deep pool, a fire, or the main hero of the chant. In Navajo legend, the Place of Emergence is where all life began. That, too, may be in the center of the painting.

When the medicine man finishes creating his painting for the day, he places prayer sticks around it. The sticks are actually reeds with pollen and fragments of turquoise inside. Pollen, which is considered sacred to the Navajo, is also sprinkled on the painting to bless it. Then the patient is called into the hogan.

The patient enters, bearing a gift of cornmeal, which is scattered as food to the painting. Then the patient undresses and is led by the medicine man to the painting. The patient sits down in the middle of it, facing east. Now the healing ceremony continues.

The medicine man sings his chant and shakes his rattle. He applies sand from the painting to the patient; in this way positive energy from the painting is thought to be transferred to the patient.

Herbal drinks may be served during the ceremony. These herbs are often gathered with special prayers and under special circumstances (for instance, one plant used in the Night Chant is picked only when lightning strikes). All herbal drinks are placed next to the sand figures before being offered to the patient, as if they come directly from the figures.

The healing ceremony ends with many puffs of smoke. Coals are lit in the hogan as a kind of disinfectant. Everyone inhales the vapors they produce.

The ceremony must be finished before sunset. Then the medicine man completely destroys the painting he has made. The beautiful colored sands are scooped up and whisked outside the hogan, to be scattered in all directions.

Soon the day's ceremonial sand painting is blown away by the wind. But tomorrow is another day. And within the Navajo medicine man's mind is a memory of how to re-create the sand painting from scratch whenever it is needed again.

THE IROQUOIS FALSE FACE SOCIETY

The Iroquois Indians of the northeastern United States and Canada are a confederation of six American tribes. They have a society of medicine men known as the False Face Society. The members of this society put on face masks which are said to have the power to cure sicknesses.

This Iroquois
False Face mask
is known as the
Harvest Mask.

Some men make their mask after seeing an image of what it should look like in a dream. They wake up and carve that image from memory on a live tree. When the carver puts the mask on his face, his personality becomes that of the mask he wears. Each mask requires much time and effort to make. When a carver is finished, other members of the False Face Society welcome the new member into their group with a great feast.

Members of the society work together to cure disease. They also perform rituals in the spring and fall. Early in those seasons, members of the False Face Society perform their traditional medicine dance. They put on their masks and ragged clothing. Then they hold a public performance, dancing and shaking their tortoise-shell rattles. Afterward, they go from house to house to eliminate evil and illness.

While outsiders to the Indian community are sometimes invited to see the public dances, they are generally not allowed to witness individual cures. However, we know that in earlier times, each patient was made to lie down next to a fire. Society members then danced around the patient, chanting songs. They scooped up hot ashes from the fire and rubbed their hands in its embers, without any sign of pain. (In their training, they learned which plants could make

their skin immune to burns.) Finally, they rubbed the hot ashes over the pained parts of the patient's body to help them heal.

Soul Retrieval on the Northwest Coast

Many different tribes exist along the Northwest Coast of the United States. Medicine people from these tribes have come to be known as shamans. This word originates from ancient people in Siberia and was originally intended for someone who was a prophet and miracle worker rather than a doctor.

Many Northwest Coast tribes believe in soul retrieval, in which the shaman goes on a "journey" to find what is wrong with the patient and the cure.

In these tribes, the shaman often makes a diagnosis by singing and dancing with a wooden rattle in order to summon a spirit helper. Sometimes the

In an Iroquois lodge, False Face masks are placed on poles while the healer chants over the patient.

whole village joins in, beating on a healer's house with poles while the healer continues dancing inside.

Finally, the shaman falls into a trance. This indicates that he is starting to contact his spirit. Some tribes believe that only by traveling to a spirit village can the shaman learn what has befallen the sick person. When the shaman comes out of a trance, he knows what the patient's problem is. Then proper treatment can begin.

Sometimes the problem is that the patient's own spirit, or soul, is missing. Perhaps a thieving spirit has stolen it. The shaman must then journey into the spirit world to track down the missing soul and retrieve it—bring it back to the sick person. Otherwise, the patient will die.

Among the Quinault, a tribe along the coast of Washington, lost souls are believed to journey along the road to the land of the dead. The only person who can recapture the soul is a medicine woman whose spirit is familiar with that road.

While lying down on a mat, the medicine woman sings a song that she has been taught in a vision. Eventually, she will go into a trance and speak with the voice of her spirit helper. Then she and her companion spirit will travel along the road to the land of the dead, with the spirit voice describing the trip.

Sometimes the medicine woman fails in her goal, but more often, she is successful. She comes back with the missing soul and symbolically pours it back into the patient's body through the top of his head.

Although this spirit flight is found all along the Northwest Coast, it is most important to the Eskimo shamans. In central and eastern Canada the shaman is known as the angakok. Here, sea animals are a major source of food. When such animals are scarce,

In Alaska, shamans wore dance aprons of buckskin painted with designs showing the spirits who were called upon to help cure the patient.

the shaman's spirit has to travel beneath the water to find Sedna, the goddess who rules these animals. The angakok's tribespeople may gather together in a dark room. There, behind a curtain, they hear their shaman's cries and calls as his spirit nears the goddess he seeks. Later, when his spirit returns, he tells everyone what has angered Sedna, and how they can appease her so that food from the sea becomes plentiful again.

THE SUCKING CURE

Among American Indians, a patient's trouble is often found to be the intrusion of a powerful object into his or her body. The object might have gotten there because the patient violated a taboo, or was "witched." Regardless of its origin, the object must be removed for the patient to get better. This often calls for the medicine person to suck it out with his mouth.

Among the Ojibwa, the medicine person might place the patient on a blanket on the floor of a wigwam. Spectators sit all around the patient, while the healer stands. A single candle may provide the only light in the room.

An Ojibwa medicine man uses a sucking tube
to withdraw the cause of illness.

The medicine person has an assistant who places
two finger-length tubes into a container that is half
filled with salt water. The tubes are made from an animal, such as a deer. They are the healer's medicine
horn. The container is placed next to the patient.

Now the assistant begins playing a drum, while
the healer sings and shakes a rattle. The medicine per-

son may also rub or blow on the patient, wave feathers, and smoke tobacco.

Then the healer kneels. He puts his medicine horn into his mouth and swallows it. Next, he vomits the horn out and uses it to suck several times around the painful part of the patient's body. Each sucking ends with his blowing through the horn into the pan of salt water. When he is finished, he signals for the drumming to stop.

The medicine person might rest for a while, then do additional sucking cures. If he is successful, he eventually spits out an object through the horn. This object is then passed around for everyone to see.

Sleight-of-hand tricks, such as a magician might use, are sometimes employed to produce objects in these sucking ceremonies by the medicine man or woman. Yet such tricks are not meant to deceive. Medicine people realize the value of a hopeful attitude. They offer their patients something they can see to help them have faith in the cure.

WITCHCRAFT

Witchcraft is a very real phenomenon to American Indians. It involves the improper use of power. Both sexes can be witches. All witches hold their ceremonies in private, unlike medicine people, who perform their rituals in public. Witches are believed able to affect whole families as well as individuals.

The Apache believe that you can avoid being "witched" by living in harmony with everyone around you. If you willingly share what you have and help when asked, you become well liked and nobody wishes you harm. Among the Apache, a witch may personally cast the "spell" or pay someone else to do it. If someone suspects that she or he has been "witched," a medicine person will be called on to discover the nature of the witchcraft. After the diagnosis, a special release-ceremony cure must be performed.

NORTH AMERICAN INDIAN MEDICAL TOOLS AND PRACTICES

Sweatbaths

Sweatbaths were required before most major tribal events. They were also the most common treatment for diseases. Sweatbaths are still used today as an important body and mind purifier. A sweatbath is taken in a sweat lodge, which is often a low, windowless hut. The material it is made from depends upon the re-

Two kinds
of Navajo
sweat houses
in Arizona.

gion. On the Northwest Coast, it is often built from wood and packed earth. In Alaska, a snow-igloo sweat lodge is used.

In some sweat lodges, the sick person enters the structure through a narrow door, then sits inside while hot rocks are inserted through an opening. Water is sprinkled on the rocks so that the hut gets hotter and hotter. Plant preparations are also frequently sprinkled on the rocks. When a patient is sweat-covered, he or she runs from the hut into the nearest body of cold water. Among the Eskimo, patients "bathe" in a heated snow igloo, then plunge into the snow outside. By friction, their bodies become warm.

Medical Charms

In a variety of regions, charms are believed able to prevent or cure disease. Some American Indians use stones for this purpose. Often with much ceremony (such as singing, dancing, and shaking rattles), these stones are placed on the unhealthy part of a patient's body.

Some tribes use arrows that are thought to possess special power. They are placed in the ground, one on each side of the patient's bed.

The Apache make a charm from the woody part of a spiny cactus known as cholla. They hang this charm around a child's neck as protection against illness. Should the whole village be threatened by an epidemic, a whole cholla might be placed in front of the community's main lodge to ward off the disease.

Medicine Bags

In all the Plains tribes and in many forest and plateau tribes, every male Native American had a medicine bag. In other tribes, women as well as men had medicine bags. This was a skin pouch containing objects believed to have great protective powers. These included herbs, roots, and other sacred things, especially plant pollen. The bags were usually made from the skin of an animal such as the otter, beaver, or mink. The more rare and hard to get was the skin, the more potent the bag was believed to be. Medicine people usually passed on their bags to one of their children, or to a favorite student.

Medicine Rattles

Rattles are used in many healing ceremonies. Hunting tribes often made theirs from the hooves or hide of deer. These were filled with beans. Farming tribes made rattles from gourds that they filled with pebbles. Other rattles were made from turtle shells, animal bladders, and leather sacks.

This Plains Indian
ceremonial bag was
made from a bison
calf's head.

An Arikara medicine
ceremony was photo-
graphed in the early
twentieth century by
Edward S. Curtis.

Water Drums

The water drum is used in many medical ceremonies. Some water drums were made from scooped-out logs. Others were made from tanned hide or large pottery jars. The base was filled nearly two-thirds full of water. A thin cured hide was stretched across the mouth. Curved drumsticks were rubbed over the drum to produce a low-pitched rumbling sound.

THE OWL PROPHET'S LAST LESSON

The Kiowa is a tribe of the plains. A famous Kiowa medicine man was known as the Owl Prophet or Do-ha-te. During the 1870s, the Kiowa united with other tribes to halt the westward advance of European settlers into Oklahoma and Texas. The Owl Prophet became the main medicine person of the tribal troops.

The Owl Prophet died a strange death. A powerful Kiowa chief known as Kicking Bird moved most of his tribe from their homeland to Fort Sill, Oklahoma, to live peacefully with the settlers. But he sent the most unruly among his warriors to be imprisoned in Florida. He believed this was for the good of his tribe.

Inside a Mandan medicine lodge, a shaman leads young participants in a traditional ceremony.

One of those he sent away was the Owl Prophet.

The laws of the Owl Prophet's medicine forbade him to kill a fellow tribesperson with his power. To break such a taboo would cost him his life. However, on the ride to Florida, another chained medicine man, named Eagle Chief, asked the Owl Prophet to pray for Kicking Bird to die soon. The Owl Prophet, still furious with Kicking Bird, did as Eagle Chief requested.

Kicking Bird was known to be in excellent health. But four days later, he keeled over in pain and soon died. When news of this reached the wagon train, the Owl Prophet knew what to expect. Sure enough, before he reached their destination at Fort Marion in Florida, the Owl Prophet too was dead. He was reported to have died from "natural causes."

MEDICINES

The forests, plains, and deserts were the pharmacies of the North American Indians. They depended upon a variety of plants to treat specific ailments and wounds. Many of these plants are still used today, and classes on how to recognize and use them are taught by Indians to Indians and non-Indians alike.

The American Indians probably learned which plants to rely upon through trial and error. Their own stomachs were their laboratories. Eventually, they developed a "doctor's kit" of healing plants in their vicinity. Sometimes they traded plants with friendly neighboring tribes.

To American Indians, when and how you harvest a plant is just as crucial as what the plant is. It is important to show respect for the plants. Therefore, they always say a prayer or make an offering when gathering a medicinal plant from Mother Earth. The offering might be a sprinkling of tobacco or corn pollen. To neglect doing so is thought to produce an illness. Medicinal plants are never to be wasted or ruined for fun.

Some of the plants used in healing ceremonies are known only to medicine men and women. However, other medicinal plants are familiar to everyone in the tribe.

Many plants used as medicines were also eaten as food. Elderberry is one exception. You wouldn't want to nibble on raw elderberries, since they may make you very sick. But cooked elderberries do make very tasty jams and jellies. And in American Indian medicine, they were a big help.

American Indians treated many diseases by having patients "clean themselves out." For this purpose, some tribes made a hot tea of the elderberry tree bark or root to help patients move their bowels or vomit. These tribes included the Iroquois, the Cherokee, and the Ojibwa. Other tribes drank a tea of elderberry blossoms as a remedy for colds and coughs. Parts of the elderberry were also made into a poultice and placed over scrapes and bruises. A poultice is a soft, sticky pad of plant or other material. It is usually heated, then put on the injured body part.

Like the elderberry, the milkweed plant should never be eaten raw. However, this poisonous plant with lovely orange-red flowers in the summer is "good medicine." Some tribes, like the Shoshone of the Great Basin, used the milkweed's milky sap as a dressing for wounds or bruises. They found it prevented infection and helped wounds heal faster. To relieve headaches, other tribes boiled a tea from its roots and washed the sufferer's head with it.

Horsemint, also known as "bee balm," is a square-stemmed member of the mint family. American Indians quickly reduced the uncomfortable pain and itching of insect bites by rubbing crumbled bee balm leaves on them.

Several tribes also used bee balm to treat wounds and skin diseases. The Winnebago of eastern Wisconsin treated acne with a tea made from its boiled leaves.

A medicine woman of western Canada.

For stomachaches and cramps, the Cherokee made a tea from the towering black birch tree. The Ojibwa used white birch for the same purpose.

For head colds, the Dakota burned the twigs of red cedar and inhaled the smoke. A Cherokee with a cold was given a drink made from willow bark. Modern scientists have learned that this bark contains a naturally occurring chemical that is similar to aspirin.

For diarrhea, many tribes relied on treatments made from chokecherry as well as wild black cherry.

For a toothache, the Iroquois and many other American Indians relied on the prickly ash, or "toothache tree." They put the inner bark of either the trunk or root of the tree directly next to the aching tooth. At other times, they sprinkled powdered bark on the sore spot. Some tribes also drank a tea made from the prickly ash's bark or berries for colds and fevers. Others gargled a tea made of the bark for sore throats. And the Fox Indians of Minnesota made a thick cough syrup by boiling down the bark with berries.

The bark of the charming pussy willow, found in swamps, as well as dry places, and thickets, was used on cuts, wounds, and bruises by some Indians. Others boiled willow tea as a hot bath for swollen feet. It was also mixed in a tea with spicewood to treat rheumatism.

The American Indians had many treatments to heal burns. These included the cattail, which was found in marshes, swamps, and ponds. The cattail's roots were pounded, then mixed with animal fat to make a burn salve.

Early European observers were impressed by the American Indians' skill in treating fractures, sprains, and dislocated bones. They made form-fitting splints out of a variety of materials, including wet clay, rawhide, and cedar. The Pima of the Southwest made their splints from the flat, elastic ribs of the saguaro, or giant cactus.

The mesquite produces beans that were the most important food for the southwestern Indians of the Sonoran Desert. This shrub was practically a pharmacy in itself. The black gum of the mesquite was boiled and used as an eyewash. It was also considered good for sore lips, chapped and cracked fingers, and sunburn. The leaves were made into a tea good for headache and stomach problems.

From the boiled root of the buffalo gourd, or wild gourd, found on dry plains and mesas of the Southwest, the Pima extracted a juice that they put in the ear for earache. Another earache remedy was used by the Ojibwa: they stewed poplar or aspen buds in bear fat to produce a pleasant-smelling ear salve.

A tea made from the berries of the bearberry or manzanita plant was used by southwestern Indians as a lotion to ease the pain of poison oak. For poison ivy, some tribes made a remedy from the leaves of the jewelweed plant.

To make childbirth easier, the Cherokee made a drink from the inner bark of black cherry, while the Zuni of the American Southwest made a drink from a small black fungus known as corn smut.

A variety of plants were used as daily tonics to prevent, rather than cure, illness. These included wintergreen and rose. The leaves of both plants were made into a tea for general good health.

In the American Southwest, the root and bark of the rose were also made into a tea for a cold remedy. Elsewhere, boiled rose root tea was used as an eyewash. The Cherokee used it for diarrhea.

This gives you some idea of the treasury of medicinal plants that American Indians knew about and used. But remember: *It is important to never sample strange plants on your own.* Experienced medicine people and explorers will tell you that. Some plants that are harmful look just like plants that are good for you. For example, carrot is good, but it looks just like water hemlock, which is deadly. It takes an experienced naturalist to know the difference.

But it is well worth learning about plants from the experts. If you can find a teacher, you are very lucky, for Mother Earth is filled with healing plants that the American Indians knew about and modern science is still using.

AMERICAN INDIAN MEDICINE TODAY

Although most people do not usually hear about them, there are still many medicine men and women living and working in North America today.

In the last few years, there has been an unusual program at Rough Rock, Arizona, which is a community near the center of the Navajo Reservation. A federal agency paid six Navajo medicine men to teach twelve young Indians the traditional ceremonies. This unique school for medicine people is part of the Rough Rock Demonstration School, the first community-controlled Indian school.

For a long time, American Indians found much to distrust in modern medicine. The concept of spirit, body, and mind interacting is basic to traditional American Indian medicine, but has not been to modern medicine. Modern medical practitioners frequently treat only the patient's body. However, the American Indian believes that the spirit of a sick person requires mending as well. Today many non-Indian health workers are recognizing the value of this approach. At the same time, many American Indians seek both modern doctors and medicine people. They feel that a combination of both types of medicine works best for them.

The Round Dance of the Cheyenne and Arapaho Indians is performed in a ceremony at Phoenix, Arizona.

Today many North American Indians use a combination of traditional and modern medicine.

When a North American Indian breaks a leg, he or she may have it set at a hospital. But the person may also want to know the spiritual reason why he broke a leg. For this reason, he or she may also call upon a medicine person. Antibiotics, a cast, and even surgery may be needed to help the patient's leg to heal physically. However, other aids are needed to heal the spirit. These may include the medicine person's herbs, songs, prayers, and ceremonies.

In recognition of their needs, many of the newer hospitals in areas where American Indians live have been designed with special rooms for ceremonies that are part of their patients' time-honored traditions.

Today, non-Indians also turn to the services and the instruction of American Indian medicine people. There are workshops and classes, magazines and books that support the study and survival of traditional medicine. Farming communities suffering through periods of drought have asked for American Indian help in bringing rain. In the 1980s, a Creek medicine man named Marcellus Bear Heart Williams was called upon to bring snow to Colorado's Copper Mountain ski resort. Sure enough, his prayers and ceremony preceded a good-sized snowfall. In medicine person tradition, Bear Heart says that he is just a caretaker and the Creator does the work of actually making it snow.

A medicine man of today participates in an annual powwow of Narragansett Indians.

There are still many mysteries to be looked at about medicine people and how they work. Perhaps these healers reach a part of the human mind in a way that we do not yet understand. In the meantime, one thing is sure: North American Indian medicine men and women are still among us, and interest in them grows.

The Navajo sandpainter, the Ojibwa Mide, the Cherokee medicine man and woman all continue to carry on the work of their ancestors. At the same time, they look for new apprentices to follow in their footsteps. They await those with true hearts, who want to become educated about harmony to themselves, their fellow people, and Mother Earth.

GLOSSARY

Angakok—an Eskimo shaman.

Apache—American Indian tribe of the Southwest.

Cherokee—American Indian tribe of the Southeast.

Chippewa—see Ojibwa.

Comanche—American Indian tribe of the Great Plains.

Creek—American Indian tribe of the southeastern United States.

False Face Society—healing group found among Northeast American Indians.

Fox—American Indian tribe of Minnesota.

Hopi—American Indian tribe of the Southwest.

Iroquois—American Indian tribe of the northeastern states.

Kiowa—American Indian tribe of the Great Plains.

Mide—Member of the Midewiwin (Medicine Society).

Midewigan—Medicine Lodge (a big wigwam) used by the Midewiwin.

Midewiwin—Medicine Society found in the Great Lakes area.

Navajo—American Indian tribe of the Southwest.

Ojibwa (Chippewa)—American Indian tribe of the Great Lakes region.

Pima—American Indian tribe of the Southwest.

Quinault—American Indian tribe of the Washington coast.

Sedna—Eskimo goddess of sea animals.

Shaman—Eskimo Medicine person.

Shoshone—American Indian tribe of the Great Basin.

Sioux—American Indian tribe of the Great Plains.

Vision quest—solo journey taken by young American Indian boys and some girls to find their guiding spirit for life.

Winnebago—American Indian tribe of eastern Wisconsin.

Witchcraft—bad use of spiritual energy.

Yurok—American Indian tribe of California.

FOR FURTHER READING

Gaddis, Vincent H., *American Indian Myths & Mysteries*. Radnor, PA: Chilton Book Company, 1977.

Hofsinde, Robert (Gray-Wolf). *The Indian Medicine Man*. New York: William Morrow and Company, 1966.

Hofsinde, Robert (Gray-Wolf). *The Indian's Secret World*. New York: William Morrow and Company, 1955.

Moerman, Daniel E. *Geraniums for the Iroquois: A Field Guide to American Indian Medicinal Plants*. Algonac, MI: Reference Publications, 1981.

Sandner, Donald. *Navaho Symbols of Healing*. New York and London: Harcourt Brace Jovanovich, 1979.

Steiger, Brad. *Medicine Power*. Garden City, N.Y.: Doubleday & Company, 1974.

▌NDEX